DreamWorks

BEE MOVIE™

MAD LIBS®

By Roger Price and Leonard Stern

W9-CKJ-748

PSS!

PRICE STERN SLOAN

PRICE STERN SLOAN
Published by the Penguin Group
Penguin Group (USA) Inc., 375 Hudson Street, New York, New York 10014, USA
Penguin Group (Canada), 90 Eglinton Avenue East, Suite 700,
Toronto, Ontario M4P 2Y3, Canada
(a division of Pearson Penguin Canada Inc.)
Penguin Books Ltd., 80 Strand, London WC2R 0RL, England
Penguin Group Ireland, 25 St. Stephen's Green, Dublin 2, Ireland
(a division of Penguin Books Ltd.)
Penguin Group (Australia), 250 Camberwell Road, Camberwell,
Victoria 3124, Australia (a division of Pearson Australia Group Pty. Ltd.)
Penguin Books India Pvt. Ltd., 11 Community Centre,
Panchsheel Park, New Delhi—110 017, India
Penguin Group (NZ), 67 Apollo Drive, Rosedale, North Shore 0745,
Auckland, New Zealand (a division of Pearson New Zealand Ltd.)
Penguin Books (South Africa) (Pty.) Ltd., 24 Sturdee Avenue,
Rosebank, Johannesburg 2196, South Africa

Penguin Books Ltd., Registered Offices:
80 Strand, London WC2R 0RL, England

Published by Price Stern Sloan,
a division of Penguin Young Readers Group,
345 Hudson Street, New York, New York 10014.

ISBN 978-0-8431-2675-4

1 3 5 7 9 10 8 6 4 2

MAD LIBS®

INSTRUCTIONS

MAD LIBS® is a game for people who don't like games!
It can be played by one, two, three, four, or forty.

• RIDICULOUSLY SIMPLE DIRECTIONS

In this tablet you will find stories containing blank spaces where words are left out. One player, the READER, selects one of these stories. The READER does not tell anyone what the story is about. Instead, he/she asks the other players, the WRITERS, to give him/her words. These words are used to fill in the blank spaces in the story.

• TO PLAY

The READER asks each WRITER in turn to call out words—adjectives or nouns or whatever the spaces call for—and uses them to fill in the blank spaces in the story. The result is a MAD LIBS® game.

When the READER then reads the completed MAD LIBS® game to the other players, they will discover that they have written a story that is fantastic, screamingly funny, shocking, silly, crazy, or just plain dumb—depending upon which words each WRITER called out.

• EXAMPLE (Before and After)

"_____!" he said _____
             EXCLAMATION   ADVERB

as he jumped into his convertible _____ and
                                              NOUN

drove off with his _____ wife.
                            ADJECTIVE

"_____*Ouch*_____!" he said _____*Stupidly*_____
             EXCLAMATION   ADVERB

as he jumped into his convertible _____*cat*_____ and
                                              NOUN

drove off with his _____*brave*_____ wife.
                            ADJECTIVE

MAD LIBS®

QUICK REVIEW

In case you have forgotten what adjectives, adverbs, nouns, and verbs are, here is a quick review:

An ADJECTIVE describes something or somebody. *Lumpy, soft, ugly, messy,* and *short* are adjectives.

An ADVERB tells how something is done. It modifies a verb and usually ends in "ly." *Modestly, stupidly, greedily,* and *carefully* are adverbs.

A NOUN is the name of a person, place, or thing. *Sidewalk, umbrella, bridle, bathtub,* and *nose* are nouns.

A VERB is an action word. *Run, pitch, jump,* and *swim* are verbs. Put the verbs in past tense if the directions say PAST TENSE. *Ran, pitched, jumped,* and *swam* are verbs in the past tense.

When we ask for A PLACE, we mean any sort of place: a country or city *(Spain, Cleveland)* or a room *(bathroom, kitchen).*

An EXCLAMATION or SILLY WORD is any sort of funny sound, gasp, grunt, or outcry, like *Wow!, Ouch!, Whomp!, Ick!,* and *Gadzooks!*

When we ask for specific words, like a NUMBER, a COLOR, an ANIMAL, or a PART OF THE BODY, we mean a word that is one of those things, like *seven, blue, horse,* or *head.*

When we ask for a PLURAL, it means more than one. For example, *cat* pluralized is *cats.*

MAD LIBS® is fun to play with friends, but you can also play it by yourself! To begin with, DO NOT look at the story on the page below. Fill in the blanks on this page with the words called for. Then, using the words you have selected, fill in the blank spaces in the story.

Now you've created your own hilarious MAD LIBS® game!

A HONEY OF A CITY

ADJECTIVE _____

PLURAL NOUN _____

VERB ENDING IN "ING" _____

ADJECTIVE _____

PLURAL NOUN _____

ADJECTIVE _____

CELEBRITY _____

NOUN _____

NOUN _____

ADJECTIVE _____

NOUN _____

VERB ENDING IN "ING" _____

PART OF THE BODY _____

SILLY WORD _____

PLURAL NOUN _____

VERB _____

MAD LIBS

A HONEY OF A CITY

Welcome to New Hive City, a/an _____ metropolis buzzing
<small>ADJECTIVE</small>

with energy and humming with _____! It is a place
<small>PLURAL NOUN</small>

of constant motion where citizens can be seen _____
<small>VERB ENDING IN "ING"</small>

along the streets at any time of day or night. _____ neon
<small>ADJECTIVE</small>

lights on the billboards, skyscrapers, and _____ along Hive
<small>PLURAL NOUN</small>

Hexagon keep the city alive at all hours. Visit the _____
<small>ADJECTIVE</small>

theater district to see such stage greats as BeeBee McGee and

_____'s _____-taming act. Go to a game at
<small>CELEBRITY</small>   <small>NOUN</small>

Buzzy Stadium where you might be lucky enough to catch a/an

_____ hit into the stands! The parks throughout New Hive
<small>NOUN</small>

City are simply _____, boasting stunning _____
<small>ADJECTIVE</small>   <small>NOUN</small>

gardens as well as paths for jogging or _____. It's
<small>VERB ENDING IN "ING"</small>

easy to get started on your tour of New Hive City. Just throw your

_____ in the air and yell "_____!" to hail one of the
<small>PART OF THE BODY</small>   <small>SILLY WORD</small>

many yellow-and-black-striped _____ zipping along the
<small>PLURAL NOUN</small>

busy streets—they'll take you anywhere you want to _____!
<small>VERB</small>

MAD LIBS® is fun to play with friends, but you can also play it by yourself! To begin with, DO NOT look at the story on the page below. Fill in the blanks on this page with the words called for. Then, using the words you have selected, fill in the blank spaces in the story.

Now you've created your own hilarious MAD LIBS® game!

SHOPPING BEE

ADJECTIVE _____

ADJECTIVE _____

VERB ENDING IN "ING" _____

PART OF THE BODY (PLURAL) _____

NOUN _____

PLURAL NOUN _____

ADJECTIVE _____

PLURAL NOUN _____

NOUN _____

PLURAL NOUN _____

PART OF THE BODY (PLURAL) _____

ADJECTIVE _____

PLURAL NOUN _____

PLURAL NOUN _____

SAME PLURAL NOUN _____

NOUN _____

PLURAL NOUN _____

MAD LIBS®

SHOPPING BEE

Barry Benson decided to go shopping at Old Buzzy, the

_____ trendy clothing store that all the _____
ADJECTIVE   ADJECTIVE

bees in New Hive City were _____ about. He couldn't
                              VERB ENDING IN "ING"

believe his _____ when he walked inside. It was like
        PART OF THE BODY (PLURAL)

a/an _____ had exploded. There were yellow and black
        NOUN

pants, shirts, and _____ in every style imaginable! Barry
                    PLURAL NOUN

tried on some _____ jeans that had _____
                ADJECTIVE   PLURAL NOUN

sewn onto them. Then he grabbed a sweater knit from the finest

_____. He added some handcrafted _____ to his
    NOUN   PLURAL NOUN

wings. *These really bring out the color of my _____!*
                                        PART OF THE BODY (PLURAL)

he thought. He even found a pair of _____ _____
                                        ADJECTIVE   PLURAL NOUN

that attached to his antennae! "Will that be cash or _____?"
                                                        PLURAL NOUN

asked the salesclerk. "_____," said Barry. He took his wallet
                        SAME PLURAL NOUN

out of his _____. *This will definitely be honey well spent,*
              NOUN

he thought. _____ *really do make the bee.*
              PLURAL NOUN

MAD LIBS® is fun to play with friends, but you can also play it by yourself! To begin with, DO NOT look at the story on the page below. Fill in the blanks on this page with the words called for. Then, using the words you have selected, fill in the blank spaces in the story.

Now you've created your own hilarious MAD LIBS® game!

U OF BEE

VERB (PAST TENSE) _____

PLURAL NOUN _____

PLURAL NOUN _____

PLURAL NOUN _____

PART OF THE BODY (PLURAL) _____

ADJECTIVE _____

VERB ENDING IN "ING" _____

PART OF THE BODY _____

PLURAL NOUN _____

TYPE OF LIQUID_____

ADJECTIVE _____

TYPE OF LIQUID _____

PLURAL NOUN _____

COLOR _____

NOUN _____

ADJECTIVE _____

"Remember our first day of college?" Barry asked Adam as

they _____ to graduation wearing their caps and
      VERB (PAST TENSE)

_____. "Sure do. Our backpacks were so heavy with all those
PLURAL NOUN

books and _____. And we wore those University of Bee
          PLURAL NOUN

_____ on our _____! But I wasn't prepared
PLURAL NOUN   PART OF THE BODY (PLURAL)

for how demanding and _____ college really was," Adam
                      ADJECTIVE

admitted. "I know," agreed Barry. "Bee _____ 101 had me
                                      VERB ENDING IN "ING"

scratching my _____ in confusion." "Well, Effective Stinging
              PART OF THE BODY

Strategies had me so stressed, I'd eat a box of _____
                                                PLURAL NOUN

every night!" Adam confessed. "And I never anticipated putting so

much blood, sweat, and _____ into those _____
                       TYPE OF LIQUID   ADJECTIVE

homework assignments!" "Yeah," recalled Barry, "I thought we'd be

sipping cups of _____ in the cafeteria or playing Frisbee
                TYPE OF LIQUID

with the other _____ on the _____ grass.
               PLURAL NOUN   COLOR

Instead, I was studying morning, noon, and _____. I guess
                                           NOUN

you could say I was as _____ as a bee."
                       ADJECTIVE

MAD LIBS® is fun to play with friends, but you can also play it by yourself! To begin with, DO NOT look at the story on the page below. Fill in the blanks on this page with the words called for. Then, using the words you have selected, fill in the blank spaces in the story.

Now you've created your own hilarious MAD LIBS® game!

HONEX'S WORK POLICIES

ADVERB _____

ADJECTIVE _____

SAME ADJECTIVE _____

PLURAL NOUN _____

ADJECTIVE _____

PLURAL NOUN _____

PLURAL NOUN _____

PART OF THE BODY (PLURAL) _____

TYPE OF LIQUID _____

VERB ENDING IN "ING" _____

NUMBER _____

ADJECTIVE _____

NOUN _____

ADJECTIVE _____

NOUN _____

NOUN _____

MAD LIBS®

HONEX'S WORK POLICIES

We here at Honex believe that if we treat our employees

_____, the results will be both _____ for
　　　ADVERB　　　　　　　　　　　　　　　　　　　ADJECTIVE

the company and _____ for our _____. To
　　　　　　　　SAME ADJECTIVE　　　　　　PLURAL NOUN

that end, we have compiled the following list of _____
　　　　　　　　　　　　　　　　　　　　　　　　　　ADJECTIVE

and effective work policies:

1) Bees shall wear clean _____ each day and always
　　　　　　　　　　　　PLURAL NOUN

　 have their ID _____ prominently displayed on the
　　　　　　　　PLURAL NOUN

　 front of their _____.
　　　　　　　　PART OF THE BODY (PLURAL)

2) Bees should get their morning cup of _____ before
　　　　　　　　　　　　　　　　　　　TYPE OF LIQUID

　 _____ to work.
　　VERB ENDING IN "ING"

3) Bees are entitled to a/an _____-minute lunch break
　　　　　　　　　　　　　NUMBER

　 during which they may either eat in the _____ room
　　　　　　　　　　　　　　　　　　　ADJECTIVE

　 or grab a quick _____ at a restaurant.
　　　　　　　　NOUN

4) Any bee who calls in _____ will be expected to bring
　　　　　　　　　　　ADJECTIVE

　 in a/an _____ from a doctor upon returning to the
　　　　　NOUN

　 _____.
　　NOUN

MAD LIBS® is fun to play with friends, but you can also play it by yourself! To begin with, DO NOT look at the story on the page below. Fill in the blanks on this page with the words called for. Then, using the words you have selected, fill in the blank spaces in the story.

Now you've created your own hilarious MAD LIBS® game!

WHAT'S THE BUZZ?

PLURAL NOUN _____

NOUN _____

TYPE OF LIQUID _____

VERB _____

EXCLAMATION _____

ADJECTIVE _____

NOUN _____

ADJECTIVE _____

ADJECTIVE _____

NOUN _____

PLURAL NOUN _____

NOUN _____

ADJECTIVE _____

ADJECTIVE _____

MAD LIBS

WHAT'S THE BUZZ?

When the workers at Honex are not as busy as _____, they
PLURAL NOUN

gather around the honey _____ with their cups of sweetened
NOUN

_____ to gossip and _____. Let's listen in ...
TYPE OF LIQUID   VERB

BUZZWELL: _____! Did you hear that Mr. Smithersbee
              EXCLAMATION

gave the _____ _____ project to
          ADJECTIVE   NOUN

Bumbleton? Sure, Bumbleton's _____, but
                              ADJECTIVE

he's a total newbee! It really bugs me!

STINGSTEEN: You think that's bad? We've got this _____
                                                   ADJECTIVE

bee in our group who thinks the _____
                                 NOUN

revolves around her.

O'HIVEY: Okay, _____. New topic. What do you think of
                   PLURAL NOUN

that new queen bee in Bee Resources? I am just over

the _____ for her! But she only has eyes for
    NOUN

McStingy. What does he have that I don't—other than

_____ looks and _____ charm?
ADJECTIVE   ADJECTIVE

FROM BEE MOVIE™ MAD LIBS® • Bee Movie TM & © 2007 DreamWorks Animation L.L.C. Published by Price Stern Sloan, a division of Penguin Young Readers Group, 345 Hudson Street, New York, New York 10014.

MAD LIBS® is fun to play with friends, but you can also play it by yourself! To begin with, DO NOT look at the story on the page below. Fill in the blanks on this page with the words called for. Then, using the words you have selected, fill in the blank spaces in the story.

Now you've created your own hilarious MAD LIBS® game!

BEES ON VACATION

VERB ENDING IN "ING" _____

VERB _____

NOUN _____

ADJECTIVE _____

PLURAL NOUN _____

PLURAL NOUN _____

ADJECTIVE _____

NOUN _____

PLURAL NOUN _____

ADJECTIVE _____

PART OF THE BODY (PLURAL) _____

SILLY WORD _____

ADJECTIVE _____

VERB _____

VERB ENDING IN "ING" _____

TYPE OF LIQUID _____

VERB _____

PLURAL NOUN _____

NOUN _____

PART OF THE BODY _____

MAD LIBS®

BEES ON VACATION

Exhausted? Stressed? _____ hard for the honey? Come

VERB ENDING IN "ING"

_____ at the Bee Resort, a five-_____ hotel

VERB   NOUN

for bees and their families. The resort boasts _____

ADJECTIVE

accommodations, including spacious _____ with

PLURAL NOUN

private bath-_____, a/an _____ view of the

PLURAL NOUN   ADJECTIVE

_____, and complimentary _____ on your

NOUN   PLURAL NOUN

pillows. The food is so _____, it'll make you clap your

ADJECTIVE

_____ to your stomach and shout, "_____!"

PART OF THE BODY (PLURAL)   SILLY WORD

But quite possibly what you'll love most about the Bee Resort are

our _____ activities: You can _____ in the

ADJECTIVE   VERB

sand all day long or go _____ in _____. Or

VERB ENDING IN "ING"   TYPE OF LIQUID

you can just _____ by the pool and soak up the sun's

VERB

_____. For all you worker bees looking to be treated like

PLURAL NOUN

the queen _____, this resort is truly the place to "bee."

NOUN

You won't have to lift a/an _____ during your stay!

PART OF THE BODY

FROM BEE MOVIE™ MAD LIBS® • Bee Movie TM & © 2007 DreamWorks Animation L.L.C. Published by Price
Stern Sloan, a division of Penguin Young Readers Group, 345 Hudson Street, New York, New York 10014.

MAD LIBS® is fun to play with friends, but you can also play it by yourself! To begin with, DO NOT look at the story on the page below. Fill in the blanks on this page with the words called for. Then, using the words you have selected, fill in the blank spaces in the story.

Now you've created your own hilarious MAD LIBS® game!

LOUNGE STINGER...
AND OTHER JOBS FOR BEES

PART OF THE BODY _____

PLURAL NOUN _____

ADJECTIVE _____

PLURAL NOUN _____

ADJECTIVE _____

PLURAL NOUN _____

VERB _____

NOUN _____

NOUN _____

PLURAL NOUN _____

ADJECTIVE _____

NOUN _____

PLURAL NOUN _____

TYPE OF LIQUID _____

NOUN _____

SAME NOUN _____

ADVERB _____

ANIMAL (PLURAL) _____

MAD LIBS
LOUNGE STINGER ...
AND OTHER JOBS FOR BEES

Barry Benson's duty as a worker bee was to make honey, but his

_____ just wasn't in it. He knew that with his skills and
PART OF THE BODY

_____ he could do non-honey jobs just as well. With
PLURAL NOUN

his _____ voice, he could be a lounge stinger and sing
ADJECTIVE

_____ like "A Bee C" by the Jackson Hive. Or, with his
PLURAL NOUN

_____ personality, he could be a beejay, spinning the
ADJECTIVE

greatest _____ and getting bees to _____
PLURAL NOUN   VERB

on the dance _____. Or maybe he'd enjoy being
NOUN

an errand bee, pedaling around on a/an _____ and
NOUN

delivering _____. He could also be an artist bee, creating
PLURAL NOUN

_____ masterpieces. Or he could be a coffee-_____
ADJECTIVE   NOUN

bee and bake fresh _____ every morning for people to
PLURAL NOUN

eat with their morning cup of _____. Or maybe he could
TYPE OF LIQUID

be a used-_____ salesbee—every bee needs a nice used
NOUN

_____! I _____ *need a new job,* thought
SAME NOUN   ADVERB

Barry. *Making honey is for the* _____.
ANIMAL (PLURAL)

MAD LIBS® is fun to play with friends, but you can also play it by yourself! To begin with, DO NOT look at the story on the page below. Fill in the blanks on this page with the words called for. Then, using the words you have selected, fill in the blank spaces in the story.

Now you've created your own hilarious MAD LIBS® game!

TO BEE OR NOT TO BEE...
A POLLEN JOCK

ADJECTIVE _____

PLURAL NOUN _____

VERB _____

ADJECTIVE _____

PLURAL NOUN _____

VERB _____

ADJECTIVE _____

NOUN _____

NOUN _____

VERB ENDING IN "ING" _____

NOUN _____

NOUN _____

NUMBER _____

PLURAL NOUN _____

PLURAL NOUN _____

PART OF THE BODY _____

PLURAL NOUN _____

ADJECTIVE _____

VERB _____

MAD LIBS®
TO BEE OR NOT TO BEE ...
A POLLEN JOCK

Wanted: Pollen Jocks

Are you a strong, strapping, _____ specimen of a bee?

ADJECTIVE

Do you crave action, adventure, and _____? Do you

PLURAL NOUN

_____ in the face of danger? Then *you* could be a Pollen Jock!

VERB

Join our team of ultra-_____ fly-_____ as we

ADJECTIVE   PLURAL NOUN

speedily _____ from the hive on _____ pollen-

VERB   ADJECTIVE

gathering missions. Win the adoration, respect, and _____

NOUN

of the bee community with your courage and _____.

NOUN

Although experience is not required, swooping and _____

VERB ENDING IN "ING"

skills are preferred. Flight gear—goggles, a fighter _____,

NOUN

and a leather bomber _____—is provided. Starting

NOUN

salary is _____ _____ a week, plus all the

NUMBER   PLURAL NOUN

_____ you can eat. If you can keep your _____

PLURAL NOUN   PART OF THE BODY

to the sky and dodge dangerous objects such as birds, brooms, bats,

and _____, then the _____ job of Pollen Jock

PLURAL NOUN   ADJECTIVE

might be right for you. _____ today for an application!

VERB

FROM BEE MOVIE™ MAD LIBS® • Bee Movie TM & © 2007 DreamWorks Animation L.L.C. Published by Price Stern Sloan, a division of Penguin Young Readers Group, 345 Hudson Street, New York, New York 10014.

MAD LIBS® is fun to play with friends, but you can also play it by yourself! To begin with, DO NOT look at the story on the page below. Fill in the blanks on this page with the words called for. Then, using the words you have selected, fill in the blank spaces in the story.

Now you've created your own hilarious MAD LIBS® game!

A BEELINE TO SAFETY

PLURAL NOUN _____

PART OF THE BODY (PLURAL) _____

NUMBER _____

NOUN _____

PART OF THE BODY _____

EXCLAMATION _____

NOUN _____

NOUN _____

PLURAL NOUN _____

PART OF THE BODY (PLURAL) _____

NOUN _____

NOUN _____

NOUN _____

NOUN _____

ADVERB _____

SILLY WORD _____

MAD LIBS®

A BEELINE TO SAFETY

On Barry's first flight out of the hive, he looked down on all the

amazing _____ in the human world and couldn't believe
　　　　　　PLURAL NOUN

his _____. He was just starting to think that leaving
　PART OF THE BODY (PLURAL)

the hive was as easy as one, two, _____ when a bright
　　　　　　　　　　　　　　　　NUMBER

_____ zoomed by, nearly clipping his _____.
　　NOUN　　　　　　　　　　　　　　　　　　　　　PART OF THE BODY

"_____!" he muttered. "That was close." He flew higher,
　EXCLAMATION

and a floating _____ on a string caught his eye. A gust of
　　　　　　　　NOUN

_____ blew it straight at him, and Barry dropped like a
　NOUN

sack of _____ to the pavement below. "What was *that*?" he
　　　　PLURAL NOUN

asked. He stood up, dusted off his _____, and turned to
　　　　　　　　　　　　　　　PART OF THE BODY (PLURAL)

see a/an _____ headed right for him. He shot up like a/an
　　　　　NOUN

_____ and nearly crashed into a flying _____
　NOUN　　　　　　　　　　　　　　　　　　　　　　　　NOUN

that two kids were tossing back and forth. Shaking, Barry landed on

the window of a parked _____. He had just caught his
　　　　　　　　　　　NOUN

breath when it started to move _____. "_____,"
　　　　　　　　　　　　　　　ADVERB　　　　SILLY WORD

Barry groaned. Time for another wild ride!

FROM BEE MOVIE™ MAD LIBS® • Bee Movie TM & © 2007 DreamWorks Animation L.L.C. Published by Price Stern Sloan, a division of Penguin Young Readers Group, 345 Hudson Street, New York, New York 10014.

MAD LIBS® is fun to play with friends, but you can also play it by yourself! To begin with, DO NOT look at the story on the page below. Fill in the blanks on this page with the words called for. Then, using the words you have selected, fill in the blank spaces in the story.

Now you've created your own hilarious MAD LIBS® game!

WHAT A GEM

SILLY WORD _____

ADJECTIVE _____

PART OF THE BODY _____

ADJECTIVE _____

A PLACE _____

NUMBER _____

CELEBRITY _____

PERSON IN ROOM _____

NOUN _____

ADJECTIVE _____

PLURAL NOUN _____

NOUN _____

VERB _____

NOUN _____

PART OF THE BODY _____

PART OF THE BODY _____

SILLY WORD _____

MAD LIBS
WHAT A GEM

The first time Ken laid eyes on the Ziamonique artificial diamonds, he

fell in love. "_____! These are simply _____!" he
　　　　　　　SILLY WORD　　　　　　　　　　　　　　　　ADJECTIVE

cried, excitedly pounding his _____ on a table. When he
　　　　　　　　　　　　　　　　　PART OF THE BODY

started selling them, he would tell people: "The Ziamonique is the most

_____ artificial diamond this side of (the) _____.
ADJECTIVE　　　　　　　　　　　　　　　　　　　　　　　　A PLACE

Everyone should own at least _____. They are especially
　　　　　　　　　　　　　　　　　NUMBER

popular with famous people like _____ and _____.
　　　　　　　　　　　　　　　CELEBRITY　　　　　PERSON IN ROOM

The Ziamonique is a girl's best _____. We have three
　　　　　　　　　　　　　　　　　NOUN

shapes: the Walnut, the Ambassador, and the Juggernaut. The Walnut

is _____ with shiny _____; the Ambassador is
　ADJECTIVE　　　　　　　　　　　PLURAL NOUN

perfect for that special _____ who likes to _____;
　　　　　　　　　　　　　NOUN　　　　　　　　　　　　　VERB

and the Juggernaut is bigger than a/an _____. The
　　　　　　　　　　　　　　　　　　　　　　　NOUN

Ziamonique is a cut above the rest, and when a guy gets down on his

_____ to ask a girl for her _____ in marriage,
PART OF THE BODY　　　　　　　　　　PART OF THE BODY

he can be assured that when she sees that rock on her finger, her

answer will be '_____, yes!'"
　　　　　　　SILLY WORD

FROM BEE MOVIE™ MAD LIBS® • Bee Movie TM & © 2007 DreamWorks Animation L.L.C. Published by Price
Stern Sloan, a division of Penguin Young Readers Group, 345 Hudson Street, New York, New York 10014.

MAD LIBS® is fun to play with friends, but you can also play it by yourself! To begin with, DO NOT look at the story on the page below. Fill in the blanks on this page with the words called for. Then, using the words you have selected, fill in the blank spaces in the story.

Now you've created your own hilarious MAD LIBS® game!

BEE MINE, BY BARRY

PLURAL NOUN _____

PLURAL NOUN _____

NOUN _____

NOUN _____

PLURAL NOUN _____

PART OF THE BODY _____

ADVERB _____

ADJECTIVE _____

PART OF THE BODY (PLURAL) _____

NOUN _____

PLURAL NOUN _____

SILLY WORD _____

PART OF THE BODY _____

PLURAL NOUN _____

ADJECTIVE _____

NOUN _____

PART OF THE BODY (PLURAL) _____

MAD LIBS
BEE MINE, BY BARRY

My dearest Vanessa, how does this bee love thee? Let me count the

_____! Your eyes are the color of _____, and
PLURAL NOUN   PLURAL NOUN

your heart is made out of pure _____. My darling snuggle-
                                        NOUN

_____, I want to whisper sweet _____ in
NOUN   PLURAL NOUN

your ear. It's a wonder you can't hear my _____ beating
                                              PART OF THE BODY

_____ whenever I am near you. If I didn't know how
ADVERB

_____ it sounds, I would tell you I am head over
ADJECTIVE

_____ in love with you. I would climb the tallest
PART OF THE BODY (PLURAL)

_____ and shout to the _____, "_____!
NOUN   PLURAL NOUN   SILLY WORD

I love Vanessa Bloome with all my _____!" If you would bee
                                        PART OF THE BODY

mine, I would shower you with the most beautiful _____
                                                    PLURAL NOUN

honey could buy. If you would give me a chance, Vanessa, this

_____ bee would bee your _____ in shining
ADJECTIVE   NOUN

armor and sweep you off your _____. What do you
                                PART OF THE BODY (PLURAL)

think?

MAD LIBS® is fun to play with friends, but you can also play it by yourself! To begin with, DO NOT look at the story on the page below. Fill in the blanks on this page with the words called for. Then, using the words you have selected, fill in the blank spaces in the story.

Now you've created your own hilarious MAD LIBS® game!

TASTY MORSELS

A PLACE _____

ADJECTIVE _____

PLURAL NOUN _____

PLURAL NOUN _____

PLURAL NOUN _____

PLURAL NOUN _____

NOUN _____

PLURAL NOUN _____

COLOR _____

NOUN _____

NOUN _____

PLURAL NOUN _____

PLURAL NOUN _____

PLURAL NOUN _____

NOUN _____

PLURAL NOUN _____

MAD LIBS®
TASTY MORSELS

"It's like you've died and gone to (the) _____," Barry told
 <u>A PLACE</u>

Adam about all the different kinds of human food. "They have food for

different moods, for _____ events, for everything! When
 <u>ADJECTIVE</u>

they're upset, they might eat frosted _____ or mashed
 <u>PLURAL NOUN</u>

_____ covered in gravy or crispy, salted _____.
 <u>PLURAL NOUN</u>   <u>PLURAL NOUN</u>

And when they're happy, they dish up these huge bowls of

_____ with whipped _____ on top. During some-
 <u>PLURAL NOUN</u>   <u>NOUN</u>

thing they call 'the big game,' they have platters of _____
                                                                    <u>PLURAL NOUN</u>

that they dunk into this _____ stuff called 'dip.' Oh, and
                              <u>COLOR</u>

they serve really yummy snacks called 'pigs in a/an _____'
                                                                  <u>NOUN</u>

and '_____ wings'! And if that's not enough, you should
     <u>NOUN</u>

see their kitchens! They have cans of _____ and boxes of
                                              <u>PLURAL NOUN</u>

_____ in their cupboards, and they keep containers of left-
 <u>PLURAL NOUN</u>

over _____ in their refrigerators, which they reheat the
       <u>PLURAL NOUN</u>

next day in the micro-_____. They probably even stash
                           <u>NOUN</u>

food under their _____. In fact, I'd bet honey on it!"
                      <u>PLURAL NOUN</u>

MAD LIBS® is fun to play with friends, but you can also play it by yourself! To begin with, DO NOT look at the story on the page below. Fill in the blanks on this page with the words called for. Then, using the words you have selected, fill in the blank spaces in the story.

Now you've created your own hilarious MAD LIBS® game!

YOU'VE GOT BEE-MAIL

ADJECTIVE _____

NOUN _____

ADVERB _____

ADJECTIVE _____

NOUN _____

ADJECTIVE _____

PLURAL NOUN _____

NOUN _____

NOUN _____

PLURAL NOUN _____

NOUN _____

NOUN _____

PART OF THE BODY _____

NOUN _____

ADJECTIVE _____

ADVERB _____

MAD LIBS®
YOU'VE GOT BEE-MAIL

Dear Barry: We have been _____ friends for so long that
　　　　　　　　　　　　　　　ADJECTIVE

I think of you as my own _____. So I feel I can speak
　　　　　　　　　　　　　　NOUN

_____ to you about your recent _____ bee-
ADVERB　　　　　　　　　　　　　　　　　ADJECTIVE

havior. I won't beat around the _____. Your crush on
　　　　　　　　　　　　　　　　　NOUN

Vanessa is inappropriate and _____. There are plenty of
　　　　　　　　　　　　　　ADJECTIVE

other _____ in the hive. Frankly, you would be better
　　　PLURAL NOUN

off falling in love with a/an _____ instead of a human!
　　　　　　　　　　　　　　NOUN

Really, Barry, you should avoid humans like the _____. I
　　　　　　　　　　　　　　　　　　　　　　NOUN

realize that life is not always a bowl of _____, my friend,
　　　　　　　　　　　　　　　　　　PLURAL NOUN

but we bees have a pretty good _____. You've got to
　　　　　　　　　　　　　　　NOUN

start "Thinking Bee," Barry! When life hands you lemons, you make

_____-ade. Am I getting through to you at all, or am I
NOUN

just banging my _____ against a brick _____?
　　　　　　PART OF THE BODY　　　　　　　NOUN

Please stop all this _____ foolishness!
　　　　　　　　　　ADJECTIVE

_____Yours,
ADVERB

Adam

FROM BEE MOVIE™ MAD LIBS® • Bee Movie TM & © 2007 DreamWorks Animation L.L.C. Published by Price
Stern Sloan, a division of Penguin Young Readers Group, 345 Hudson Street, New York, New York 10014.

MAD LIBS® is fun to play with friends, but you can also play it by yourself! To begin with, DO NOT look at the story on the page below. Fill in the blanks on this page with the words called for. Then, using the words you have selected, fill in the blank spaces in the story.

Now you've created your own hilarious MAD LIBS® game!

MUST-BEE TV

NOUN _____

ADJECTIVE _____

VERB _____

ADJECTIVE _____

PLURAL NOUN _____

TYPE OF LIQUID _____

NOUN _____

VERB ENDING IN "ING" _____

PLURAL NOUN _____

ADJECTIVE _____

PLURAL NOUN _____

ADJECTIVE _____

ADJECTIVE _____

VERB _____

MAD LIBS®
MUST-BEE TV

After the five o'clock _____ rings and every bee
                         NOUN

heads home from a/an _____ day at work, they like to
                          ADJECTIVE

_____ in their _____ Lazybee recliners, relax,
     VERB   ADJECTIVE

and watch a little TV. They make bowls of delicious _____,
                                                        PLURAL NOUN

pour tall glasses of _____, and tune in to see their
                      TYPE OF LIQUID

favorite shows. *HoneyBob BeePants* is about a bee who lives in a/an

_____ under the sea. *Bee Idol* showcases the _____
   NOUN   VERB ENDING IN "ING"

talents of bees who want to be singing _____. *Extreme*
                                          PLURAL NOUN

Makeover: Hive Edition is a/an _____ reality show where
                                    ADJECTIVE

hives are redecorated with beautiful _____. The MTBee
                                        PLURAL NOUN

channel is very _____, especially with teen bees. *BEE!*
                    ADJECTIVE

True Honeywood Stories features interviews with celebrity bees

and in-depth looks into their _____ lives. And one of the
                                 ADJECTIVE

longest-running shows, which bees stay up late to watch, is *Saturday*

Night Hive, a bee-loved comedy show that will make you laugh until

you _____!
       VERB

FROM BEE MOVIE™ MAD LIBS® • Bee Movie TM & © 2007 DreamWorks Animation L.L.C. Published by Price
Stern Sloan, a division of Penguin Young Readers Group, 345 Hudson Street, New York, New York 10014.

MAD LIBS® is fun to play with friends, but you can also play it by yourself! To begin with, DO NOT look at the story on the page below. Fill in the blanks on this page with the words called for. Then, using the words you have selected, fill in the blank spaces in the story.

Now you've created your own hilarious MAD LIBS® game!

VANESSA'S DIARY

ADJECTIVE _____

NOUN _____

ADJECTIVE _____

PLURAL NOUN _____

VERB ENDING IN "ING" _____

NOUN _____

ADJECTIVE _____

PART OF THE BODY (PLURAL) _____

NOUN _____

NOUN _____

ADJECTIVE _____

TYPE OF LIQUID _____

NOUN _____

ADVERB _____

ADJECTIVE _____

MAD LIBS
VANESSA'S DIARY

Dear Diary: Today the strangest thing happened. Ken was about to

hurt a/an _____, defenseless bee, but luckily I was able to
              ADJECTIVE

open the _____ and let the _____ bee outside.
              NOUN   ADJECTIVE

After Ken left, I decided to wash the _____. As I was
                                          PLURAL NOUN

_____ to the sink, I heard something. It sounded like
VERB ENDING IN "ING"

someone talking, but no one else was in the room. The sound was

coming from the _____. When I went to investigate, I
                      NOUN

found only the _____ bee I had rescued a few minutes
                    ADJECTIVE

ago. And then I saw it with my own two _____—that
                                            PART OF THE BODY (PLURAL)

bee started talking and thanking me for saving his _____! I
                                                        NOUN

thought for sure I was headed straight for the loony _____,
                                                          NOUN

but then he talked some more. He's a really _____ guy. His
                                                ADJECTIVE

name is Barry. We talked and told jokes for hours over hot, steaming

glasses of _____ and pieces of _____. He
              TYPE OF LIQUID   NOUN

makes me laugh so _____. It's always nice to make a/an
                        ADVERB

_____ friend—even if that friend is a bee!
ADJECTIVE

FROM BEE MOVIE™ MAD LIBS® • Bee Movie TM & © 2007 DreamWorks Animation L.L.C. Published by Price Stern Sloan, a division of Penguin Young Readers Group, 345 Hudson Street, New York, New York 10014.

MAD LIBS® is fun to play with friends, but you can also play it by yourself! To begin with, DO NOT look at the story on the page below. Fill in the blanks on this page with the words called for. Then, using the words you have selected, fill in the blank spaces in the story.

Now you've created your own hilarious MAD LIBS® game!

NOW I'M A BEE-LIEVER

VERB ENDING IN "ING" _____

NOUN _____

PLURAL NOUN _____

NOUN _____

ADJECTIVE _____

VERB _____

NOUN _____

NOUN _____

ADJECTIVE _____

NOUN _____

ADJECTIVE _____

PART OF THE BODY _____

ADVERB _____

NOUN _____

NOUN _____

PART OF THE BODY _____

NOUN _____

MAD LIBS®
NOW I'M A BEE-LIEVER

Barry knew he and Vanessa couldn't be together, but that didn't stop

him from day-_____ about it. Their perfect date would
           VERB ENDING IN "ING"

go like this: First he'd fill a picnic _____ with cheese and
                                 NOUN

_____. Then he'd put on his favorite black-and-yellow-
   PLURAL NOUN

striped _____—the one that made him look rugged and
            NOUN

_____. When he was ready, he'd _____ over to
ADJECTIVE   VERB

Vanessa's _____, hover under her window, and serenade her
           NOUN

by playing a/an _____ and singing a/an _____
                 NOUN   ADJECTIVE

song like "You Are My _____-shine." When she came
                       NOUN

outside, Barry would tell her how _____ she looked
                         ADJECTIVE

before taking her by the _____ and _____
                PART OF THE BODY   ADVERB

escorting her into his sporty little _____. He'd take her
                       NOUN

to Sweet-_____ Field in the park, where he'd confess to
        NOUN

her how near and dear to his _____ she was. Sure, it's just
               PART OF THE BODY

a/an _____, but a bee can dream, can't he?
     NOUN

FROM BEE MOVIE™ MAD LIBS® • Bee Movie TM & © 2007 DreamWorks Animation L.L.C. Published by Price
Stern Sloan, a division of Penguin Young Readers Group, 345 Hudson Street, New York, New York 10014.

MAD LIBS® is fun to play with friends, but you can also play it by yourself! To begin with, DO NOT look at the story on the page below. Fill in the blanks on this page with the words called for. Then, using the words you have selected, fill in the blank spaces in the story.

Now you've created your own hilarious MAD LIBS® game!

GET YOUR BLOOD PUMPING WITH MOOSEBLOOD

PART OF THE BODY (PLURAL) _____

NUMBER _____

PLURAL NOUN _____

PART OF THE BODY (PLURAL) _____

NOUN _____

ADJECTIVE _____

PLURAL NOUN _____

PLURAL NOUN _____

PLURAL NOUN _____

ADJECTIVE _____

VERB _____

PLURAL NOUN _____

NOUN _____

ADJECTIVE _____

ADJECTIVE _____

NUMBER _____

MAD LIBS®
GET YOUR BLOOD PUMPING
WITH MOOSEBLOOD

"Drop to your _____ and give me _____!"
                    PART OF THE BODY (PLURAL)   NUMBER

barked Mooseblood the Mosquito. "You're not bugs, you're slugs! You

move like old _____. You'd lose your _____
                  PLURAL NOUN   PART OF THE BODY (PLURAL)

if they weren't attached." It was the first grueling day of

_____ Camp, where bugs from all over came to participate
     NOUN

in Mooseblood's _____ fitness regimen for staying
                    ADJECTIVE

safe against windshield wipers. Mooseblood, a master at avoiding

disaster, flexed his _____, cracked his _____,
                     PLURAL NOUN   PLURAL NOUN

and eyed his students. "Wake up and smell the _____!
                                              PLURAL NOUN

When you go up against one of those _____ wipers,
                                    ADJECTIVE

it's either do or _____!" he snarled. To prepare them for
                  VERB

wiper-survival, he made his students lift _____, run ten
                                          PLURAL NOUN

laps around the _____, and follow a/an _____
                NOUN   ADJECTIVE

liquid diet. After all, no pain, no gain, and Mooseblood had to live up

to his guarantee—a/an _____ body in _____
                      ADJECTIVE   NUMBER

days or less or your honey back!

MAD LIBS® is fun to play with friends, but you can also play it by yourself! To begin with, DO NOT look at the story on the page below. Fill in the blanks on this page with the words called for. Then, using the words you have selected, fill in the blank spaces in the story.

Now you've created your own hilarious MAD LIBS® game!

HIVE AT FIVE

ADJECTIVE _____

ADJECTIVE _____

NOUN _____

ADJECTIVE _____

NOUN _____

NUMBER _____

NOUN _____

ADJECTIVE _____

ADJECTIVE _____

PLURAL NOUN _____

PLURAL NOUN _____

PERSON IN ROOM _____

NUMBER _____

NOUN _____

PLURAL NOUN _____

PLURAL NOUN _____

MAD LIBS
HIVE AT FIVE

Good evening. This is Bob Bumble with *Hive at Five*, your

_____ action news source. Our top story tonight is a/
ADJECTIVE

an _____ honey spill along Pollen Parkway. This sticky
ADJECTIVE

situation resulted when a/an _____ carrying honey
NOUN

collided with a/an _____ _____, causing it
ADJECTIVE   NOUN

to overturn. The flooding honey has caused a/an _____-
NUMBER

_____ pileup on the parkway. There was some
NOUN

_____ stinging and name-calling, but so far there
ADJECTIVE

are no reports of any casualties. The driver of the tankard is in

_____ condition after being ejected and landing in a pile
ADJECTIVE

of _____. _____ are on the scene. In sports,
PLURAL NOUN   PLURAL NOUN

_____ has been chosen as the number _____
PERSON IN ROOM   NUMBER

draft pick of the Honeycombs, the Yankbees' Class B farm

_____. On the weather front, it will be cloudy tomorrow
NOUN

with a chance of thunder-_____. And that's the news for
PLURAL NOUN

tonight, folks. Good night—and good _____.
PLURAL NOUN

FROM BEE MOVIE™ MAD LIBS® • Bee Movie TM & © 2007 DreamWorks Animation L.L.C. Published by Price Stern Sloan, a division of Penguin Young Readers Group, 345 Hudson Street, New York, New York 10014.

MAD LIBS® is fun to play with friends, but you can also play it by yourself! To begin with, DO NOT look at the story on the page below. Fill in the blanks on this page with the words called for. Then, using the words you have selected, fill in the blank spaces in the story.

Now you've created your own hilarious MAD LIBS® game!

STINGER MANAGEMENT

ADVERB _____

ADJECTIVE _____

ADJECTIVE _____

ADJECTIVE _____

ADJECTIVE _____

NUMBER _____

NUMBER _____

VERB ENDING IN "ING" _____

TYPE OF LIQUID _____

PLURAL NOUN _____

ADJECTIVE _____

NOUN _____

NOUN _____

NOUN _____

ADJECTIVE _____

SILLY WORD _____

SAME SILLY WORD _____

SAME SILLY WORD _____

MAD LIBS®
STINGER MANAGEMENT

Stinging is usually fatal for bees—but, fortunately, Adam recovered

_____. After his _____ operation, Adam
　　　ADVERB　　　　　　　　　　　ADJECTIVE

decided to devote his life to teaching a/an _____ course
　　　　　　　　　　　　　　　　　　　　　　　ADJECTIVE

in stinger management. He prepared a/an _____ list of
　　　　　　　　　　　　　　　　　　　　　ADJECTIVE

things for bees to do when they become angry and are in danger of

losing their _____ tempers:
　　　　　　　ADJECTIVE

1) Count from _____ to _____ while
　　　　　　　　　NUMBER　　　　　　　　NUMBER

_____ deeply.
VERB ENDING IN "ING"

2) Drink a cup of steaming _____ made with lots of
　　　　　　　　　　　　　　TYPE OF LIQUID

honey to calm your _____.
　　　　　　　　　　PLURAL NOUN

3) Write a/an _____ letter to the person who upset you,
　　　　　　　ADJECTIVE

then promptly throw the letter into the _____.
　　　　　　　　　　　　　　　　　　　　　　　NOUN

4) Take a long walk around the _____ to clear your
　　　　　　　　　　　　　　　　　NOUN

_____.
　　NOUN

5) Go into a quiet, _____ room, close your eyes, and
　　　　　　　　　ADJECTIVE

chant:"_____, _____, _____."
　　　　　SILLY WORD　　　　SAME SILLY WORD　　　SAME SILLY WORD

MAD LIBS® is fun to play with friends, but you can also play it by yourself! To begin with, DO NOT look at the story on the page below. Fill in the blanks on this page with the words called for. Then, using the words you have selected, fill in the blank spaces in the story.

Now you've created your own hilarious MAD LIBS® game!

SHOW ME THE HONEY

ADJECTIVE _____

EXCLAMATION _____

PLURAL NOUN _____

NOUN _____

NOUN _____

VERB ENDING IN "ING" _____

NOUN _____

PART OF THE BODY _____

PLURAL NOUN _____

VERB ENDING IN "ING" _____

PLURAL NOUN _____

ADVERB _____

NOUN _____

NOUN _____

PLURAL NOUN _____

PART OF THE BODY (PLURAL) _____

NOUN _____

MAD LIBS®
SHOW ME THE HONEY

The _____ ATF&H agents swarmed before Barry, awaiting
        ADJECIVE

orders. "_____!" he commanded. "Listen up, _____!
      EXCLAMATION   PLURAL NOUN

Here's what we've got! Our operation today is dubbed Code

_____. Our orders are to seize every last _____
    NOUN   NOUN

of honey the humans have, whether it's _____ on
                                       VERB ENDING IN "ING"

supermarket shelves or being squeezed onto _____
                                         NOUN

nuggets. Keep your _____ to the ground for any tea
                   PART OF THE BODY

parties little _____ may be having. If you hear anyone
           PLURAL NOUN

_____, check their cough _____. If someone's
VERB ENDING IN "ING"   PLURAL NOUN

hair smells _____ sweet, check their shampoo. Leave no
           ADVERB

_____ unturned! Now remember, we'd prefer not to use
    NOUN

force with the honey thieves, but we will if we have to. If you get

into trouble, pick up your walkie-_____ and call for backup.
                                 NOUN

Fasten your _____ and keep your _____
         PLURAL NOUN   PART OF THE BODY (PLURAL)

inside the vehicle at all times. C'mon, guys, let's get this _____
                                                 NOUN

on the road!"

FROM BEE MOVIE™ MAD LIBS® • Bee Movie TM & © 2007 DreamWorks Animation L.L.C. Published by Price
Stern Sloan, a division of Penguin Young Readers Group, 345 Hudson Street, New York, New York 10014.

MAD LIBS® is fun to play with friends, but you can also play it by yourself! To begin with, DO NOT look at the story on the page below. Fill in the blanks on this page with the words called for. Then, using the words you have selected, fill in the blank spaces in the story.

Now you've created your own hilarious MAD LIBS® game!

FLIGHT OF THE FLOAT

NOUN _____

VERB _____

NOUN _____

PLURAL NOUN _____

NUMBER _____

COLOR _____

NOUN _____

NOUN _____

PLURAL NOUN _____

NOUN _____

PERSON IN ROOM _____

PLURAL NOUN _____

NOUN _____

MAD LIBS®
FLIGHT OF THE FLOAT

Barry and Vanessa had to get the Princess and the Pea float on a/an

_____ to New York if they wanted to save the flowers. "It's
    NOUN

not going to _____ on my parade—not today!" yelled Barry
       VERB

as Vanessa veered the float onto the freeway. The _____
                                      NOUN

that Vanessa wore on her head flew off. Barry glanced back and

saw it get crushed by oncoming _____. That's when he
                                PLURAL NOUN

noticed the _____ other floats cruising behind them. The
               NUMBER

_____ Riding Hood float swerved to avoid a/an
   COLOR

_____ in the road. The sudden movement knocked the Big
  NOUN

Bad _____ overboard. He landed on a clothesline on the
       NOUN

Emperor's New _____ float, causing a _____
                 PLURAL NOUN   NOUN

to fly off and hit the driver of the Hansel and _____ float.
                                    PERSON IN ROOM

The driver hit the brakes, and the house made of _____
                                     PLURAL NOUN

toppled off the float and onto the freeway. *It's like watching a/an*

_____ *in a china shop*, thought Barry, *only much, much*
    NOUN

worse.

FROM BEE MOVIE™ MAD LIBS® • Bee Movie TM & © 2007 DreamWorks Animation L.L.C. Published by Price
Stern Sloan, a division of Penguin Young Readers Group, 345 Hudson Street, New York, New York 10014.

This book is published by

PSS!

PRICE STERN SLOAN

whose other splendid titles include such literary classics as

The Original #1 Mad Libs®
Son of Mad Libs®
Sooper Dooper Mad Libs®
Monster Mad Libs®
Goofy Mad Libs®
Off-the-Wall Mad Libs®
Vacation Fun Mad Libs®
Camp Daze Mad Libs®
Christmas Fun Mad Libs®
Straight "A" Mad Libs®
Pirates Mad Libs®
Family Tree Mad Libs®
Mad Mad Mad Mad Mad Libs®
Mad Libs® On the Road
The Apprentice™ Mad Libs®
Austin Powers™ Mad Libs®
The Powerpuff Girls™ Mad Libs®
Scooby-Doo!™ Mad Libs®
Madagascar™ Mad Libs®
Over the Hedge™ Mad Libs®
Teen Titans™ Mad Libs®
Fear Factor™ Mad Libs®
Fear Factor™ Mad Libs®: Ultimate Gross Out!
Survivor™ Mad Libs®
Guinness World Records™ Mad Libs®
Betty and Veronica® Mad Libs®
Napoleon Dynamite™ Mad Libs®
Nancy Drew® Mad Libs®
The Mad Libs® Worst-Case Scenario™ Survival Handbook
The Mad Libs® Worst-Case Scenario™ Survival Handbook 2
Shrek the Third Mad Libs®

and many, many more!
Mad Libs® are available wherever books are sold.